iMATTER

26 AFFIRMATIONS FOR GIRLS AND BOYS

Building Self-Esteem
through the ABC's of Life

Kesha Nichols

3G Publishing, Inc.
Loganville, Ga 30052
www.3gpublishinginc.com
Phone: 1-888-442-9637

First published by 3G Publishing, Inc., January, 2017.

ISBN: 978-1-941247-34-1

Printed in the United States of America

Contents

From the Author

Thank you so much for wanting change so much that you picked up this book. I salute you and dedicate this book to YOU. I applaud you for taking this first step while on your journey to healing and transformation.

I myself was bullied and there were days that I wanted to give up and hurt others because I was in pain and hurting but that was not who I am, so I never acted upon it. There was something deep inside of me that said no Kesha you are worth much more. I am somebody and iMatter.

I say to you Beloved that you matter; say it with me loud and clear "iMatter!" To me YOU do matter.

Kesha Nichols

Introduction

This book grew out of my participating in Career Day at a public elementary school. I posed the following question to the students, "If you were to write your own book today what would be the title of your book?" A beautiful little girl wrote BULLY on her paper. I looked at her paper three times and asked her if BULLY was the title of her book and she responded, "YES". Well, this ripped to the core of my heart and I immediately knew that day that I had to do something and by that evening this book was lifted from my soul.

Bullying is a nightmare that children live with every day at the hands of their parents, siblings, classmates and peers. This issue must be addressed in a manner that enables children to report this kind of abuse without the fear of retaliation. iMatter will be a tool to reach around the world to empower children with the knowledge essential to their survival when faced with bullying. It's time to save our children!

iMatter – 26 Affirmations for Girls & Boys has 26 affirmations and affirmation for each letter of the alphabet, an affirming word for the day with the definition of the word and is accompanied by a journal.

Building Self-Esteem through the ABC's of Life

AFFIRMATION FOR TODAY

ACCEPTANCE

Being accepted starts with you first. Know that you have so much to offer.

Say it with me "I have so much to offer" repeat it over and over until you believe it.

A – Acceptance

IDENTIFY: I accept me for who I am. No longer will I look to others for acceptance or validation.

AFFIRM: Today I agree with you that you are acceptable, just the way that you are.

Acceptance- (1) favorable reception, approval (2) the act of accepting or the state of being accepted or acceptable.

A

AFFIRMATION FOR TODAY

BEST FRIEND

You have so much to offer, your kindness and charming personality. I am more than confident that before you know it you are going to have true genuine friendships.

Say it with me "To have one best friend is all that I need."

B – Best Friend

IDENTIFY: Today I will be my own best friend first. Opening the opportunity for me to have meaningful relationships.

AFFIRM: Today I agree that you are your own best friend first then others will follow.

Best- (1) of the highest quality, excellence, or standing (2) most excellently or suitably.

Best Friend – (1) the one friend who is closest to you.

B

AFFIRMATION FOR TODAY

CONQUEROR

You have the ability to overcome any obstacle, this I know for sure. You were born with great strength, that's what makes you more than a conqueror.

Say it with me "I am more than a Conqueror."

C – Conqueror

IDENTIFY: I believe that I can do anything that I put my mind to. I am more than a Conqueror!

AFFIRM: Today I agree that you can conquer anything that stand in your way of greatness.

Conqueror – (1) to overcome, defeat (2) to overcome (an obstacle, feeling, desire, etc.).

C

AFFIRMATION FOR TODAY

DOMINION

Today I challenge you to take dominion over your doubt and walk into your destiny. I believe that you were born with such greatness for the world to see.

Say it with me "I have Dominion and there is a great destiny for my life, no doubt or fear can hold me back."

D – Dominion

IDENTIFY: I will no longer walk in doubt but walk in faith believing I have dominion over everything.

AFFIRM: Today I agree that doubt is no longer an option in your life because you have dominion over it. Say it loud and clear I have Dominion!

Dominion – the power to rule, having control, authority or influence.

D

Celebrate Having Authority

AFFIRMATION FOR TODAY

ENCOURAGE

When you learn how to encourage yourself then you allow the door to open for others to encourage you as well.

Say it with me "I will first Encourage myself so that I can be able to Encourage someone else."

E – Encourage

IDENTIFY: I will learn how to encourage myself, when no one else is around to encourage me.

AFFIRM: Today I agree that you can encourage yourself and always stay encourage, think positive.

Encourage - to inspire with courage, spirit or confidence.

E

AFFIRMATION FOR TODAY

FEARLESS

You are exceptional which makes you fearless. Know that you were created to be a champion, to be the best at whatever you are created to be. You cannot let fear stop you.

Say it with me "I Am Fearless!"

F – Fearless

IDENTIFY: I will say to myself each morning that I am Fearless and Fearfully made.

AFFIRM: Today I agree with you that you are fearless and fearfully made. There is no one like you; you are hand crafted by God.

Fearless – (1) unafraid, bold, brave, courageous (2) invulnerable to fear or intimidation.

F

Celebrate Your Fearlessness

AFFIRMATION FOR TODAY

GIFT

Gifts come in all shapes and sizes. Many times the best gifts are unexpected. You are an unexpected gift ready to be unwrapped for the world to see.

Say it with me "I am a Gift" I am the best gift anyone can have as a friend, brother, sister, son or daughter...I AM A GIFT!

G – Gift

IDENTIFY: I am a gift to be unwrapped for others to see my greatness.

AFFIRM: Today I agree with you that you are a gift for the world to see and unwrap.

Gift – a special ability or capacity, natural endowment, talent.

G

AFFIRMATION FOR TODAY

HAPPY

We all deserve to be happy. My happiness starts with me. Close your eyes and think about only good things, the things that make you happy. Now what makes you happy? What do you see?

Say it with me "I Am Happy" starting today my happiness starts with me.

H – Happy

IDENTIFY: I deserve to live a happy life today and every day forward.

AFFIRM: Today I agree that happiness will now be a part of your life starting today.

Happy – (2) delighted, pleased, or glad (2) feeling, showing, or expressing joy, pleased.

H

AFFIRMATION FOR TODAY

INSPIRED

Your inspiration comes from within. What inspires you; to help others, to care for animals, to help cook dinner or plant flowers in the yard. Whatever inspires you be the best at it. You already have greatness in you.

Say it with me "I Am Inspired to be the Best _______"

I – Inspired

IDENTIFY: I am inspired to make new changes in my life and build new friendships.

AFFIRM: Today I am inspired about your new changes in your life.....for change is good.

Inspired – as an influence, feeling, thought, or the like does.

I

AFFIRMATION FOR TODAY

JOYFUL

I have Joy Joy Joy down in my heart, these are the words to a song and how true these words are. Your heart is full of joy and each day you have the choice to live a joyful day.

Say it with me "this world did not give me my joy and this world cannot take it away"

This Joy is mine….Oh Yes It Is!

J – Joyful

IDENTIFY: I deserve to live a joyful life and no one can take it away.

AFFIRM: Today I agree that each day forward will be a joyful day for you.

Joyful – full of joy, elated.

J

AFFIRMATION FOR TODAY

KIND

I believe that being kind will get you far in life. To do a kind act usually is not so much for the person receiving but for the person giving. I read that people who volunteer or do daily acts of kindness live longer healthier lives than those who do not. I volunteer faithfully. Today do something kind, acts of kindness will always come back to you.

Say it with me "I Am Kind and I deserve to be treated with Kindness."

K – Kindness

IDENTIFY: Kindness will follow me where ever I go. I deserve to be treated kind.

AFFIRM: Today I agree that you deserve to be treated with great kindness.

Kindness – (1) the practice or quality of being kind (2) a kind, considerate, or helpful act.

K

AFFIRMATION FOR TODAY

LOVE

You are so loved, that's why I wrote this book, yes for you. I promise you that you will see that there are many others that feel the same way about you.

First it starts with you, say it with me "I Am Love say it again I Am Love one more time I Am Love. Yes, you are."

L – Love

IDENTIFY: I am Love so I give it and I expect to get it in return.

AFFIRM: Today I agree that you will walk in love and love will come back to you in return.

Love – (1) out of affection or liking (2) infused with or feeling deep affection or passion.

L

AFFIRMATION FOR TODAY

MIRACLE

I believe in miracles and I believe that miracles happen every day. When a baby is born that's a miracle. I know that you believe in miracles because you are a miracle; which makes you extra special.

Say it with me "I am a Miracle."

M – Miracle

IDENTIFY: I believe that I am a walking, living, breathing miracle. Yes I am a Miracle!

AFFIRM: Today I agree that you are a miracle.

Miracle – (1) a person or thing that is a marvelous example of something (2) a wonder, marvel.

M

AFFIRMATION FOR TODAY

NON – NEGOTIABLE

There are certain things in life that are negotiable, who I am and my great worth is not one of them. I am non – negotiable.

Say it with me "I am worth more than any material thing; you cannot put a price on my worth. I am valuable, I am PRICELESS. I am Non – Negotiable!"

N – Non-Negotiable

IDENTIFY: iMatter and who I am is non-negotiable. My value and worth can't be negotiated.

AFFIRM: Today I agree that you do matter and that's non-negotiable.

Non - a prefix meaning "not".

Negotiable – mutual or discuss on, arrangement of the terms of an agreement.

N

AFFIRMATION FOR TODAY

OVERCOMER

I can overcome any obstacle that come my way. I have great inner strength to overcome any challenge or situation that I face.

Say it with me "I am an Overcomer."

O – Overcomer

IDENTIFY: I can overcome any obstacles that come my way.

AFFIRM: Today I agree that you have the ability to overcome any and all obstacles, challenges and problems in your life.

Overcome – succeed in dealing with a problem or difficulty.

O

AFFIRMATION FOR TODAY

PURPOSE

What do you believe that you were created to do? Do you know that you have a purpose in life, what do you think that purpose is? Although you may be young, you are still important enough to do something extraordinary.

When you realize what that purpose is, you are going to make a difference in the world.

Say it with me "I have a great Purpose and I am going to be a world changer."

P – Purpose

IDENTIFY: I was created with a great purpose and destiny for my life.

AFFIRM: Today I agree that God's purpose for your life is far greater than you can ever imagine for yourself.

Purpose – (1) The object toward which one strives or for which something exists; an aim or a goal (2) determination, resolution.

P

Celebrate Your Purpose

AFFIRMATION FOR TODAY

QUALITY

You are not junk but you are great, you are of quality. Do not let anyone tell you anything different, a classmate, a family member, a teacher and even a parent. You are the crème dela crème, you are all that and then some more.

Say it with me "I am better than average, I am great Quality."

Q – Quality

IDENTIFY: I deserve the best quality of life that I so richly was created to have.

AFFIRM: Today I agree that your great qualities will be known to others, no more accepting crumbs.

Quality – (1) a distinguishing characteristic, property, or attribute (2) degree or standard of excellence, a high standard.

Q

43

AFFIRMATION FOR TODAY

REMARKALBE

Look in the mirror do you see how remarkable you are? Trust me those who do not like you it's surely because they don't like who they are and they don't have what it takes, they don't even come close to your greatness.

Say it with me "I am Remarkable, I am an original and that makes me one of a kind."

R – Remarkable

IDENTIFY: I am an original and that makes me remarkable.

AFFIRM: Today I agree that you are remarkable. There is nothing common or ordinary about you. Truly one of a kind.

Remarkable – (1) worthy of being likely to be noticed especially as being uncommon or extraordinary (2) worthy of attention.

R

AFFIRMATION FOR TODAY

SPECIAL

There is only one you, not even twins are created alike, each of us have our own identity, personality, gift and talent. That is what makes us all special; there is a small group who are extra-special, just extra-ordinary. I believe that you are that small group.

Say it with me "I am extra-special, just extra-ordinary. "

S – Special

IDENTIFY: I am special; I was born with a unique purpose and plan for my life, which makes me extra-ordinary and one of a kind. I Am Special!

AFFIRM: Today I agree with you that you are special and God has a great plan for your life.

Special – (1) better than ordinary (2) distinguished, set apart from, or excelling others of its kind.

S

AFFIRMATION FOR TODAY

TREASURE

You are a priceless treasure. There is so much to be said that is great about you. Erase every negative thought or mean thing that people may have said to you or about you. None of it is true, you are a jewel, and a treasure to behold.

Say it with me "I am a Priceless Treasure".

T – Treasure

IDENTIFY: In me is a hidden great treasure that is PRICELESS.

AFFIRM: Today I agree that you are a treasure to be found by others your worth is valuable you are Priceless.

Treasure – a thing or person that is highly priced or valued.

T

AFFIRMATION FOR TODAY

UNIQUE

Look in the mirror behold the beauty that come from the inside out. You are an original; there is no one that beat you at being you. You cannot be duplicated, you are unique, one of a kind for sure.

Say it with me "I am an original that makes me quite Unique."

U – Unique

IDENTIFY: I am unique, my uniqueness is a gift, ready to be unwrapped for the world to see.

AFFIRM: Today I agree that your uniqueness will shine bright for the world to see. Only you can do what you do...You Rock!

Unique – being the only one of a particular type, single, sole (2) without equal or like; unparalleled.

U

AFFIRMATION FOR TODAY

VICTORY

I believe that there is nothing that you cannot overcome. You have the victory over every problem or situation that comes your way.

Say it with me "I have the Victory; I can NOT be defeated."

V – Victory

IDENTIFY: I have the victory over all challenges or problems that I may face.

AFFIRM: Today I agree with you that you have the victory to overcome any challenge or problem. You are victorious!

Victory – a success attained in a contest or struggle or over an opponent, obstacle or problem.

$\mathcal{V}$

AFFIRMATION FOR TODAY

WISDOM

In all things use wisdom, using wisdom is key in all of your decision making. Making wise choices in life will take you places you never dreamed about. It will open doors to great possibilities beyond your imagination.

Say it with me "I will use Wisdom in everything I do especially in choosing friends."

W – Wisdom

IDENTIFY: I will use wisdom in choosing my friends.

AFFIRM: Today I agree that being wise in choosing your friends is key, no longer accepting negative people. You will no longer let others chose you but you chose them. You make the choice of who you call friend.

Wisdom – the ability or result of an ability to think and act utilizing knowledge, experience, understanding, common sense, and insight.

W

AFFIRMATION FOR TODAY

X-FACTOR

I truly believe that the person reading this book was born with great significance. One to be celebrated. In a few words, you are an X-Factor.

Say it with me "I am an X-Factor and one day my name will be great and known for making a significant mark in the world."

X-Factor

IDENTIFY: I am great; I am an X-Factor!

AFFIRM: Today I am agreeing with you that you are great and a world changer; you are truly an X-Factor.

X-Factor – a noteworthy special talent a quality (2) a variable in a given situation that could have the most significant impact on the outcome.

X

AFFIRMATION FOR TODAY

YOUTHFUL

Enjoy your days of young. You have so many great experiences to look forward to. Do not let anyone stand in the way of your dreams and aspirations. Your life matters, YOU matter. Enjoy each day and every day that you are giving thanks. No matter how old you may grow to become always be youthful at heart.

Say it with me "iMatter and each day is a day to be celebrated."

Y – Youthful

IDENTIFY: The world needs to know that young people have feelings to and that we matter. Enjoy these years of your youth. iMATTER!

AFFIRM: Today I agree that you may be young but you do matter, you matter to me. Your youthful years are the best years of your life. Enjoy and live them well.

Youthful – having or showing the freshness or energy of someone who is young.

y

AFFIRMATION FOR TODAY

ZEALOUS

I know that deep inside of you is a zeal to make a major impact in this world. After all you are a world changer.

What are you most passionate about; take that positive energy and make a difference an impact in someone's life. I'm more than confident that you can and that you will.

Say it with me "I am Zealous about life and I am going to make a mark in this world."

Z – Zealous

IDENTIFY: I am zealous about living a life full of possibilities, greatness, purpose and with true friends.

AFFIRM: I totally agree with you that your new zealous attitude will change your life for the better.

Zealous – filled with or inspired by intense enthusiasm or zeal.

Z

Celebrate Your Zeal

JOURNAL

How has my affirmation inspired me today?

____

____

____

____

____

____

____

____

____

____

____

____

RESOURCES

Youth Frontiers, Inc.
6009 Minneapolis, MN 55416
Youthfrontiers.org
Phone Number 888-992-0222

Not In Our Town
P. O. Box 70232
Oakland, CA. 94612
Info.niot.org
Phone Number 510-268-9675

Make Beats Not Beat Downs
Makebeatsnotbeatdown.org
mbnbd@hotmail.com

Stop Bullying
stopbullying.gov

Pacer's Center, Inc.
National Bullying Prevention Center
8161 Normandale Blvd.
Bloomington, MN. 55437
pacer.org
bullying411@pacer.org

Megan Meier Foundation
515 Jefferson Suite A
St. Charles, MO 63301
Meganmeierfoundation.org
info@meganmeierfoundation.org
Phone Number 636-757-3501

Do Something
19 West 21st Street, 8th Floor
New York, NY 10010
dosomething.org
help@dosomething.org
Phone Number 212-254-2390

Children With Out A Voice
Ambassadors 4 Kids Club
P. O. Box 4351
Alpharetta, GA. 30023
info@a4kclub.org
Phone Number 404-474-4020 Ph. 800-999-9999 (for
children) Ph. 800-422-4453 (for parents)

Ground Spark
901 Mission Street, Suite 205
San Francisco, CA 94103
info@groundspark.org
Phone Number 800-405-3322 Ph. 415-641-4616

Champions Against Bullying
championsagainstbullying.com

The No Bully System
1014 Torney Avenue
P. O. Box 29011
San Francisco, CA. 94129
Phone Number 415-767-0070

Stomp Out Bullying
stompoutbullying.org
Phone Number 877 (NO BULLY) 602-8559

Angels Hope Australian Anti Bullying Organization
Angels4olivia.org

Up Stand in New Zealand
upstand.org
Phone Number 800 – kids line (800 54 37 54)